T	H	E
S	Q	U
A	R	E

THE SQUARE

❋

LYTTON SMITH

NEW MICHIGAN PRESS
TUCSON, ARIZONA

NEW MICHIGAN PRESS
DEPT OF ENGLISH, P. O. BOX 210067
UNIVERSITY OF ARIZONA
TUCSON, AZ 85721-0067

<http://newmichiganpress.com>

Orders and queries to <nmp@thediagram.com>.

Copyright © 2021 by Lytton Smith.
All rights reserved.

ISBN 978-1-934832-78-3. FIRST PRINTING.

Design by Ander Monson.

Cover photo 171560009 © Pavel Nadelyayev | Dreamstime.com

CONTENTS

The Square   1

Acknowledgments   43

...afterness, in which what has superseded or outlived remains intricately indebted to the very thing it has outlived or overcome. There can be no after without a debt, an unsettled relation, a haunting. It is to this constellation of the after that the present book returns again and again...

—Gerhard Richter, *Afterness*

"The people want the president to be honored!" they yelled, a variation on a popular chant that started in Tunisia and spread around the region, about the people wanting the government to fall.

"The people want the president put on trial!" yelled back an impromptu counterdemonstration that the police kept across the street.

—*New York Times*, March 25th, 2011

Law 107 (2013). The following text has been decided. Citizens have the right to organize and join peaceful public meetings and protests. A public meeting is every gathering in a site entered by or could be entered by individuals without a prior personal invitation, not less than ten to discuss or exchange views on an issue of general interest. A protest is every gathering of individuals not less than ten in a public place or square to express opinions, demands, or political discontentment peacefully. Participants in public meetings and protests are prohibited to disrupt public security or hamper citizens' interests or affect the course of justice, public utilities, roads, water, or air. Whoever wishes to organize a public meeting or protest should submit a written notification to the police station or point that falls within the zone of the public meeting or protest. The notification is to be delivered by hand at least three and not more than fifteen working days before. The Minister of the Interior or specialized Director of Security may issue a justified decree prohibiting or suspending or relocating the public meeting or protest. Participants are prohibited to carry incendiary material or to wear masks or coverings to hide facial features. Officially dressed security forces may disperse the public meeting or protest: firstly, requesting from the participants to voluntarily depart; secondly, in the case of non-responsiveness, in the following order, using water cannons, tear gas canisters, batons; and, in the case of the failure of the previously stipulated methods, firing warning shots, sound bombs, gas bombs, rubber cartouche bullets, non-rubber cartouche bullets, and tools proportionate to the danger posed against life, money, or property. Specified safe areas may be determined in front of vital facilities such as premises of governmental, military, security and auditing agencies, hospitals, oil facilities, museums, monumental areas, and other public facilities; participants are prohibited from trespassing the boundaries of the specified safe areas. This law shall be published in the Official Gazette and be enforced one day following the day of its publishing.

What are the people demanding?	The people want the president to be honoured; or, the people want the president put on trial.
When did the people come?	Last Friday. Or we've been here the whole while starting to make projects. Or we came when other protesters threatened to cast the president from his home; the president looks after the people.
Why have the people come?	Because the word flicker doesn't call to mind a firefly's night playfulness but the dim humming of our useless stoves in summer brownouts.
What do the people want?	Not just the truth but to have our teeth back in our mouths. A health service, jobs, and schools.
How long will the people stay?	We have our tents. Our children are trying out the diphthongs and cadences of activism. Power strips are charging our mobile devices.
What will people do after?	Democracy. Vote. Show that the people's voice is never hoarse, or harsh. Or return to any homes and jobs and lovers left to us. To brownouts.
Who have the people lost?	A co-worker, batoned. A niece, gone missing. A childhood friend, spun by sniper fire. An aunt who disagrees with us. How it feels to be at liberty.
What are the people hoping?	That the square will be circled in a chant that sounds the larynx of the nation.

       the square
its assembly
       takes shape in time   and space
                                          entering through
in theory the square   huddled alleyways, paths
       is as public   warrened via the crevices
as any voice is and   of apartment buildings
       always belonged to   the agents of the police
the citizens   are hidden inside
                                          the buildings
                                          that surround the square

       but who can say
who are citizens   whisper whips the crowd
             the state   the police have beaten down
with its participatory democracy   the inner walls of enclosing
       and the stamp of passports,   buildings, the police are in the square
               fingerprints   as much as the protesters are
the headshot on an identification card   the police are here to protect
a driving license   and serve the citizens

              or the way a trashcan with wood
              paper and other incendiary material
              stuffed down into it conflagrates
              heat tender enough to bring people closer
              even knowing there can be no closure—

                                          even knowing there can be no closure—

In the weather of the square, lightning
blues sky down to flagstones. The density

of the atmospherics enough in theory
to alter the keeping of time, to perceptibly

shift perception from caryatids and porticoes
to weatherweight. Weather the original pathos

instrument signalling guttural roar, ominous
rumble. Lightning blues sky down etc. Static

charges the air of the square into motion,
sparking with energy. Colder now, surer

of itself, the square. Barometric pressure
rising, gusts tugging at the pamphlets

scattered about the square encampment.
Something building and already begun.

The protests do not emerge from a void. Cellular conversations, a network of phones around the city. Status updates; evites. In person, on a bridge leading into a square, a string of words passes into an aerosol of breath but not before percussing the ear drums of two or three others. A tremor of rumour. A gathering organizes itself in the square as if the square assembles the gathered. What is in the air is a desire for people to talk to other people. A woman cooks trays of pasticcio and brings them, and as people come to eat, they talk. In the air the smell of ziti, of beef sauce, of bechamel sauce sprinkled with feta and gruyère. A hunger in the air and people wanting to talk rather than just shout or march. Wanting to put their lives on hold. Either there are tents or people go home to their beds and assemble again in the square in the days after. Detritus burns in oil barrels to keep the participants warm when the sun declines behind the square's erosion-wearied buildings, which might comprise hotels, a museum, bureaucratic offices, residential dwellings, religious centres, a historic and heavenly gate, public restrooms. The flagstones or cobblestones or grass of the city square—perhaps a circle or polygon or rectangle or park, any agora or forum where well more than ten are now a camp, an assembly, a participatory democracy with votes and microphones and working groups and dissent and sexual assault and bricks and voices raised to drown out other voices—disappear beneath the feet and groundsheets of all those the square has gathered. At the square's centre is the statue of a general or an ancient tree (perhaps an oak) or a water feature such as a fountain or bird bath. Here a makeshift podium has been set on a bolted-together stage and the gathered create human corridors to and from it. In the absence of electricity or voice amplification devices, the singular echo of individual voices takes any one person's words outwards, a kind of Brownian motion for the citizenly potential of the larynx, of fingers signing the words anyone here has for the future. For what will come when the gathering is broken up and citizens are in thereafter.

The square is a container in which particles and bodies disperse. The word for this, pedesis, is a word for leaping. For what feet might do, given a square, given a gathering, forgiven the usual rules of squares. Do Not Swim In The Fountain. Do Not Pick The Flowers. Occupancy By More Than Ten Persons Without Permit Is Prohibited. In the air as in the square bodies mingle in multitudinous ways, their dancing in reality a revelation of matter in motion, matter previously invisible to the eye, matter in the form of bodies moving of their own accord. The bodies which are least removed from their neighbours jostle, set to motion by repeated unseen blows that cannon them against other, heftier bodies until a movement mounts up and gradually rises to the level of the senses. An agitation. Brownian motion. Bodies in motion, bodies moved by blows. The collision of two equal but opposing forces contained within a square—an effervescent kinesis towards a change in state. The rule of law seeks a stasis that the laws of science indicate pedesis can no more rut into than metaphor can resist its own translation from one way of being in the world into another. For the particles to remain contained within the square nothing must be broadcast from it. Bodies must be beaten back and down. The excited must be subdued.

How is everyone here   hearing this,
the hiss-scuff of skittering CS gas canisters,
the leashed pressure of safetied water cannon
in the hands of government agents strategically
positioned in the upper stories of the square's
Brutalist architecture, their blood diffusing
the same oxygen as the protesters below.
An audible drumming thrums, layered
.wav files of adrenaline heartbeats, of tanks
rumbling their approach in bass along
the square's connector roads and bridges?

To be reading this is to already know
how it ends. The lit touchpapers,
the begetting of trouble. Thereafter.

Bricks hefted into palms. Hands fabricating
against tear gas makeshift masks. As cloths
to face coverings so coups to democracy.

Some of the dictatorships get thrown over
and all the states become more repressive after.
A carting away of bodies, a breaking down

of tents, camps, and gatherings into pieces.
Why occupy a square and what quadratic
equations, what geometry, might rescue

each square's 8-day or x-day collective
from utopia as much as from nostalgia?
After, in the squares where bullet holes

pock buildings, and out beyond them
where the populace is more placid now,
can what lingers beyond the barricades be

hand gestures staying it all, cupped palms
holding the heat of a fire or sound to an ear?
Speech from hand and mouth towards whomever might hear on the square's other sides?

When the first of the lachrymatory agents wheezes into smokescreen,

Gas! Gas! Quick! the protesters hunker against the museum's

orange-soda outer walls. Their handkerchief masks thin to gauze.

Sandstone abrades their fleshy torsos, hemmed there in the square

the way one hundred years ago their grandfathers retched, bodies

wrenching in mud-walled trenches in the service of the world's

metropolitan generals. To make someone else weep, first you must

release for them 2-chlorobenzalmalononitrile ($C_{10}H_5ClN_2$). The protesters

splutter an agony of cries that get heard on public service broadcasts,

protest movements shared in living rooms worldwide while the protesters

bathe their eyes in Coke®, fumble to share a balm of halved onion

with a stray police officer caught amid the exploded canisters. The protesters

are on their knees in the square. It looks like prayer twisted by oppression.

Still no damages have ever been awarded to those sprayed with tear gas.

The square is plural first person pronoun.
It gathers people in real time. The citizens,
occupiers and protesters with their chants

and handed-around poems; military humans;
the governmental will of the people and
despite the people; the radio audiences

wirelessly connected. And text, which in
this facsimile square points towards a gutter
like drainwater slicking the cobblestones.

Rainfall is a soundbed to this and all that
will come in thereafter after this—the overthrow
of the dictator can be simultaneous with the

suppression, incarceration, and/or disappearance
of those who, right now, before the after, are here
in the square. The radio audience disappears, too,

a hand turning a dial like the pages of newspapers
or an anchor turning now to the next foreign
correspondent. All the corresponding squares

and events over on the airwaves, all the pages.

& someone is handing out coupons, a voice

says, look, there, coupons for hand-stitched

clothes, for manual labour and getting paid

for manual labour, and for childbirth, coupons

for orgasms and for laughter, for the body to

release itself into convulsion, when and where

would one redeem it, what does one do with

what is just paper, no longer even plant matter,

and what is the economy of paper, the ecology

of this unwarranted handing out of quadrilaterals

of paper, fragments that promise whomever is holding

this paper is holding in their hands an experience

in words they had not thought they could ask for

and must pass on, or cash, or let drift to the gutter.

                Reports rumour in   around and from
the square, flitting   in and out   of earshot
            There has been an attempt   to enter the Great Hall   of the people.
                    A citizen was   burned to death
by ruffians staying in the square.   Is the only way left
        retreat. Citizens and students tried   to stop   23 guns, some bombs
            the army shot the students and the citizens.
                                            They were simply ignored even

Many armored vehicles   there was gunfire their clothes
        stained with blood   people were trying to talk
            citizens and students tried   tired   to stop
to stop   tear gas towards the people
        around the square
            corpses were lying   all over the square

        there was no response
                            no one stayed in one place the whole night
too much to remember   everything in the square
clearly
        a critical moment
                                        a prison, a prism
                                        an abattoir
                                        charnel-house
                the lights in the square have gone out
and must while saluting the republic
the fate of those killed or wounded   who saw a lot ignored
this broadcast contained the hard facts
                            the square being cleansed of its discontents—

there are on the bridge into the square—
exposed—protesters—say that a bridge—
might sing, that wind through the arches—
might fret itself into expression—some hum—
low and becoming words—how else to know—
the stories of the hundred and rising gunned—
down—if not that girders have their dirges—
a hundred heavenly so, and gone—abutments—
span—ricochet—sniperfire—hollowbullet—
some song beyond pockmark & bullethole—
the accumulated sonic energy of suspension—
wires—of gunfire—say that a bridge might—
sing—say that soundwaves never die out—
that footfall is a counterpoint—choreograph—
the bridge's apron, its sag and saddle—say—
a bridge might be more than dead bodies—
dropped—from railings like so many potato sacks—
a song that rails—there are protesters—there—
on the bridge—the dirge—on the bridge—
there are protesters only if the sounds of them—
the sounds—persist—not just of them gunned—
down—the sound—holds—

At night, the air cools,
right by the ground, the local temperature

the protesters at rest
in tent nylon with the handing out of poems

and glances, and after
the sun goes down, after all there is is moon

lit by reflection
and fragile in its light, the sandstone cold

to hands, to bodies &
when otherwise it should not be possible

to hear them, voices
fetch, soundwaves that bend down into

an afterless cold, voices
audible out there, traveling through media,

voices beyond their source
and out of time, how long ago these voices were,

voices from which square,
how soon they will be gone to thermal equilibrium,

voices from bodies gone
cold, gone from the square   and into thereafter

Whether and how the square changes the future depends also on what happens outside the square. When security agents disperse the camps, breaking and bending tentpoles so they cannot hold anything up, ripping canvas so it cannot keep out the elements, some protesters will head home to a district in the city's north-west quadrant. Finding an open window in the defunded library, eight of them will enter. They will sleep there, among the handful of pulpy, dog-eared bestsellers with broken spines left for some reason on the emptied-out shelves. Come the light of morning, they will open up to the public, manually stamping and lending the books to anyone who asks. When the council calls them squatters, they will call themselves community librarians. When the council plans to sell the site to a developer, local residents will ballast the library, bringing books in their hundreds and thousands to repopulate the shelves. When the council yields, the community librarians will pop a champagne bottle and continue with rotas and library cards, reading and talking. With the project of turning a shuttered building's open window into a meeting place that, from the right angle, resembles a public square or park or other space set aside for citizens to gather.   Back in the present tense, prefigurative, the protesters are still in the square, in the moments before thereafter. If they are free to come and go, to leave would be to hand the space to the state. When they are kettled in with barricades, water cannons, and gas canisters they cannot lob back fast enough to stop cyanocarbons riddling their bodies with sobs, the protesters' only escape routes are images, audio broadcasts, social media, #tags. The square gathers a collaborative. A collaborative of squares—a spring of squares—gathers a movement, momentary, precipitous. Think of a figure with a plastic shopping bag in each hand wandering into a tank's path and stopping its tracks. Not moving on. An antistasis as calm as breath or voice should be. How the square changes the future depends also on what's outside the square, whether anyone's listening to or seeing or broadcasting this.

Things can't stay the same after this. The story was written after the collapse, it was the day after, after a militia unit opened fire on a crowd, on the morning after, in the days after the strike, after Friday prayers, square after square fell to the protesters, in the months after the dictator's fall, less than seven weeks after, after a series of diplomatic appointments, after the shutdown, after all people wanted to join in, after victory, shortly after, one day after, similar marches started after prayers, after a pretty dismal decade, massive demonstrations after, after the first few years, after the January massacres, after all, revolutions began to fray soon after, after being expelled from, sexual harassment became routine again in the months after the protests.

In thereafter theory, protesters   shift from bodies to corpses

    to the ghost actions of citizens   & ghosts become more persons

than afterimages. This theory   acknowledges bricks, teargas

    riot shields, gasmasks fabricated   with fabric. What comes after

is a debt the way an equal &   opposite reaction is a debt,

    two offbalance elements   propped into equipollence.

When thereafter theory passes   into praxis the square becomes

    a museum then a mausoleum,   artifacts & bodies & cracked

stone. An unsettling afterimage.   A museum of the square, time

    & dislocation, the disrememberment   of the history of history.

Where this ends the museum   knows as little as a mausoleum

    knows of death, which is   containment, which is public square,

is print and broadcast media   modulating the voice of the people

    for the archive. For display.   For an afterlife, a halflife, of bodies.

What would it take for the square
to be temporary? To take a square
flagstone from its bed & transplant?
To plant in this emptiness an oak,
a cupule holding an oak nut, seed
encased, a figuration of the future?
What comes next in the sequence?
In the game of the will of the people
the dictator congratulates the people
on the oak he planted and the people
purport to have gathered to watch
it blossom. Makebelieve the statue
of the famous general remembers
his deeds of national consequence
and not his desire for reanimation
in quicklime. For the square to be
temporary someone has to break
with the status quo. To anticipate
the change beyond and to humour
the prelude. To unmask the dictator
even if it means uprooting the oak.
When the state retaliates in the form
of Common Protected Areas where
it commits to safeguard the wildlife,
protesters leave specified safe zones

to hunt down the species the state
has sanctioned. Such is the logic
of resistance and survival towards
resistance. The gathered remaining
inside the institution even if they've
dismantled the walls and strung up
the corpses of lynxes and ocelots.
For the square to be temporary
there must be a public that works
to disassemble the notion of a public
the state can live with. The earth
is one measure of the cost. If the oak
at the square's centre stands ceremonial
and historic, encircled by a neat fence,
the occupation becomes a dataset
for the square's successful rehabilitation
as a civic park. Where everyone goes.
No matter there are bodies dragged
away along gravel paths: the square
is uninterruptible and the protesters
need it still standing for it to be occupied.
Occupied, it continues to stand for
the state to say the city is still stable.
There's an oak growing at the centre.
An ache. Correct the record: an oak.

How and why cities made of their public spaces
squares that were circles and trapezoids is a story

lost to history. But in the squares of this spring
rising up a geometry extends, the way parallel lines—

for example the edges of a page—will extend
around the world beyond the thought of today

and back to themselves. These discrete squares, circles
and rotaries, arteries where people in circulation

span out into the city and future, touch. The state
wants geometry ordered, has ordered all benches

removed, the square made inhospitably public.
Geometry teaches instead how to come to a point,

a use of space equilateral and ancient. How citizenly
it would be tonight to speak together a geometry,

to measure together the earth. To make a movement.

The square tonight is the square of jurisdictions.

Audible under its porticoes is the aftersound

of a village, pintoresco, quaint in the latelight,

bombarded. Flattened by a gravity that pulls dropped

bombs along. By echoing machinegun reap which sows

the azure-capped fields with village bodies. The square

tonight is an oak shattered and fuero and hissing.

Is the way distance mutes gore. The way a disaster

passes into art. And, years down the line, tourists

reverent and respectful tune in for the afterechoes

one might imagine reveberate long after a period

of exposure. The square, tonight its own demesne,

sets its own law: the people's soundbed shall patter

with weaponry and yet be processed as downpour.

The square causes a causality it cannot anticipate.
Like the sun's passage from the square's east road in
to its west road out, that causality has a parabola.

Like the parabola of a dance partner's upper torso
swung down to hang their head dangerously low.
Like the parabola of an arm swung at the shoulder

releasing a ball or a canister towards the crowd. One
in play and jest, one in play towards distress. What
a gas. What a lark. Like a song sung so far away

from inhalation. Like bars wavering semibreves
on the breeze as a burst of toxins momentarily
leads the body to shut down its sensory systems.

Tears flow, a precursor to inflamed ducts, to rent
ligaments, taut ligatures, to the body unable to hold
within itself its own liquid. Unable to contain itself,

welling blood up a discoloration pressuring the skin.
The body letting the world play out in [inaudible].
The body in spasms on the paving stones as the senses

blur back and on the air can be heard the clave of salsa,
drifting amid the smoke wisps dissipating. The guests
in the hotel several streets away are learning to dance

and sound travels through media such as the day's stillness.
The percussion of the song's 1-2-3, 1-2, 1-2-3, 1-2
reverberating its cause-and-effect, tinny with distance.

For what's eroded softly underfoot
can't be retrieved. Even a shadow
obscures an image. The fracture
of a patterned tile and something

is missing from this picture. Sun
seems to arc the square as if nothing
on earth is moving. Shadow telling
the time of the uprising by where

it lines the square's colonnades.
The shadow lengthening as Earth's
revolutions turn the square away,
as fleeting as the dictator's regime

given enough bodies, given time
& human frailty. In the meantime
light, then shadow, breaks on the backs
of the crowd. Nothing gets more

visible. Nothing as light as the dust
that shuffling feet rub from flagstones.

In the absence of votes, or voices, a system of education or health, in the absence of being able to come and go from the square or being able to leave the square into an after in which the dictator will be the human megaphone of the people's army, the protesters labour to dismantle the monumental statue at the centre of the public square. The history of power is the history of such disequilibrium of statues, the dissolution of which can be expressed by the quadratic equation $ax^2 + bx + (c \times d) = 0$, where a is the relative anger of present humans, b is the bulk of the statue in question, c is the determinable size of the crowd, and d is the usefulness of tools that are to hand. Solving for x is an exercise in square movements. Bare hands may be enough but ropes, especially ropes tied to the rear fender of a vehicle in the rare circumstances in which a vehicle has been allowed within the square and close to the statue, can haul down quartzite figures, given enough hands and hatred. Where hatred is a factor in the equation for dissolution, that statue's fate has a distributive probability of rubble, of being broken back from art and terror to rock, irregular, and earth.

                                                                              the protests scatter
                                  the protesters   in the wake of the police
                       raised voices   the uprising   here where
              the roads delta out, an estuary   of fleeing people
    at maidan   along instytutska street   the elevated bridge
                   where bricks neat fit hands where bricks slug
         air towards the gathered below   what punctuates
                                 a silence spacious as white noise
                       after the fall about to be happening
              in government square   stretching the length of avenue habib bourguiba
not the fall of the bricks
                  taksim square   valiasr square
                      not yet, not the fall, yet, of heads   of state   here
pearl roundabout   here where was before the cleansing
                              a monument of six sails holding up a sphere
        the fall of the cement arch crushing a migrant crane worker in the haste
        to tear down, the fall
                     haft-e-tir square, azadi square
                  at army checkpoints   and back on the bridge   the bricks
their parabolas predictable   liberation   time, and again   the bricks
(and the poems, and songs)   revolutions, green, past tense of the dictator particular
           what surges in the moments after, the excitement
enqelab square   or an emptiness, awaiting
present tense of the dictator particular
                               in readiness,   there   all along the bridge
                  bricks, fit into hands, neat as riot gear, as an architecture
                  tearing itself back into the contextless fragments of mosaic

On hiatus from what's to come the air holds:
material enough to hold the weary gathered up.

Weeks into their time in the square the air holds
the birds the protesters watch up above the square.

Holds them in outstretched pose, not gliding, not
biding, just held feather & hollowbone, musical

quarter rests, poised at the edge of thereafter.

[For what comes next to happen these things have to happen first.]

    The body of the Ayatollah lies in glass then is wrapped in a white burial shroud, coming late to, trying to rewind, causality.

    Someone hunched at an enlarger in a room, working with negatives.

    Memory frays its weft stitches; something else being remembered.

    Magic lantern theatre. Civic forum. Revolution woven in the face-to-face method.

    The body of the Ayatollah in an open coffin falls or is pulled from its resting place.

    The distribution of images which, in capturing the past, seem to project the future, larger in size than the prints and yet not to the scale of life.

    The point at which the coffin overbalances. The fatal crush on the terraces. Shootings after people are herded into the stadium.

    Out-of-towners arrive at gates having been thrown open, hauled down. Someone drives the cab of the future towards the city.

    Air waves democratized and catchy as the familiarity of pop music, of commercials.

    Sound, a pressure moving longitudinally, its vibrations deconsolidating further from the source.

    Flatbed-adapted tricycles come to wheel away the bodies before the cameras.

as the crowd mills
                                        the square, its geometrics, its quadrants
        voices can be heard in wireless spaces, headphones
                                        a voice right in an ear
                because antennae   right inside the head
                because sound travels   of a distant listener
        coming over clear   is a pressure, pulsating

as the crowd mills
                                        bearing inked placards, implacable

        there is a paper record   an archive
                pulping, with its effluence
                sloughed away into water

                                        the pick of paper measuring
                                        how much ink the page hosts
        what a city absorbs by way of people

                                        its narrative

as the crowd mills
                                        the square long after being dispersed
        voices can be heard/there is a paper record
                        because .wav stores audio bitstreams
                        because paper adheres ink
                what is happening now in the past is the future thereafter
                                        voices languishing, language
                                        inextinguishable & in the cloud.

Then wind, or the sound of wind, catches sound
up. The birds above: an arrow, a migration awaiting
the gathered after the square becomes less the police,
the counter-protesters, suburban bliss & doldrums,
& instead oceans, flight across oceans in overloaded
boats the birds will see like tesserae, fragments
of a larger, colourful, disintegrated image. To see
as the birds see—the square's pixelated grid,
how far flung are its individual atoms, its bodies,
those still breathing, those not beaten down into
limestone flagstone, to see over time those bodies
dispersed over & into water, so many molecules
in agitation at events set moving long before them—
the human eye cannot do it. When sound forces
the eardrum, listen. The report of the toppled statue.
A volcano heard three thousand miles away as
a cannon's crack. The protesters on the airwaves,
their words crossing ocean waves their bodies
couldn't pass over.

The square is a collective noun of soundscapes.
A dust of sound kicked up rising an orison.

An omni-directional microphone picking up signals
from tent homes, drumbeats, baton clashes. Not knowing

whether being recorded means passing into an archive,
into governmental memory, or else emerging, part-

scrambled, from tinny speakers into a future voices
and bodies in their gestural language fumble for

wards to. Contained in the square, these sounds
broadcasting yet never themselves leaving.

                                              Beyond,

above, out past the troposphere, there are human
voices somewhere in space, pressed to phonograph,

travelling in heliosheath, interstellar, and why won't
voices surge from the square, fetch up in an ear's funnel,

navigate the external auditory canal to disturb some
anyone's tympanic membrane?

The residue of the sound of the square :: static.
What is being heard of the square :: a colonial

soundscape still :: public service broadcasting
begun on shortwave in anglophony ("a world

service for men & women so cut off by snow,
by desert, by sea, that only voices out of the air

could reach them") sound is not :: enlightenment
(Mission to the Dark Continents™)   sound is

alter/nation, is oscillations in pressure over time
in milliseconds, is the compression of individuals

into sonic energy. Sound the distance to an ear
from an external world too urgent and near

to be seen or stomached. Sound might pluck
the body's sinews :: discordant harmonic. Might

lose the speaker's material being while freighting
their essence in pitch, amplitude and frequency.

Might be all that's left of the square, of the ways
out of the square and the past and its colonnades.

After the square there will be the promise
of voting, of a voice. To vote will be to pull
a lever, the body's jointed elbow bending
at the hinge as ligaments contract the biceps
with the machine. Exercising the triceps &
the right to vote, to a voice. The voice
wants it known it is a partial enchantment,
characteristic of an individual & broadcast
into the day's sun for others' ears. The voice
realizes it is not a voice but the larynx's
strung enunciation, glottal and gasping,
an experience of moving air, a pronounced
echo. Say kettle. Say a protests tests resting.
Say the pot calls the kettle veto. The voice
says it is also the body's motions. The voice
says so with the body's fluent hands &
in the throats in the square in a coil within
a radio's variable capacitor tuner. The voice
says it is a voice when words are an escape
when airflow, when a lowering of pressure.
The voice says in chant the chant is meant
to carry & the break of the voice, the moment
at which the body breaks but the hands do not
stop signing or singing. How bodily our
metaphors for articulation are, the voice says,
all a matter of jointing, of bones & ligaments.
The voice would say the voice cannot say
while the body is still, with a vote & no voice.

The square is, tonight, in the infinitive case.
Unlimited. The square expresses its purpose

to those who'll listen. To be here is to rearrange
the social contract with the dictator even if he's

not listening. To gather is to hustle together
an acquaintance with strangers who want to want

the same thing. The square tonight wants to express
its actions in an abstract, general way so as to preserve

and disperse them widely: To protest is to change
the world; to listen is to enlighten oneself. The square

knows to sigh with the breaths of an encampment,
to sigh the hum of charging cellular devices.

The square knows the abstract exists in order to
remove the protests from the site. To conceal

the missing. To miss the concealed the square
would have to have a case other than the infinitive.

Would have to untangle itself from elliptical questions
into the conditional mood, where tonight the protesters

                                                         would be rising and irrepress-

ible.

The square is tonight a typography,
is an alphabet, a reader wanting
the pages' ink to smudge off
and to lift inkfingers to ears
and press them close as protesters,
to hear whether ink in any language
could press voices through print,
here, set in truetype, far beyond
a square that was once a traffic circle
a square before parliament a square
whose name sounds like a reaching out,
like turning a page into the air, mayday,
moi aidez maidan, this day in may
the square has become documentary
& so filmic, so stilled images, a DVD.
The square has margins for a perimeter.
Has gutters and spines and its binding
comes in the form of injection moulded
nylon cable ties. The square is tonight
whatever the square is before being pulped.

In accordance with the law
on gatherings

(NO MORE THAN 10
WITHOUT PERMIT)

This started out as
a documentation

of the events transpiring in
several squares, parks
and other civic spaces
over a period of forty years
(a little longer than my life
lived thus far) a record
durable in the way type is

but pages, too, are partial
and the way ink bleeds
is less metaphor than
an ignorance. Sound alters
with temperature, with
the media it passes through.
Why occupy the page's thought
with a square? Who can say
who in the square are citizens.

and seeking to demarcate
the space
& constraints

of the assembly of
concerned citizens
their names &
occupations &
times they have coveted
littered, spat on
the cobbles, spat out
the dictator's name

seeking to dissent
in the full sun
of the public &

the dusty hallways of
forms-in-triplicate &
governmental file cabinets

Let the jussive. Let hypothetics. Let us
look behind the building's façade to return
the story to before its start. Let statues
taken down let in a history. Let the day
as it begins bud the tree this one last time
before wind brings it down. Let numbers
in equations stand for bodies and let breaths
rise and fall and rise in the place of bodies.
Let movements cause, let cause produce
the body that says, too far, now, too far. Let
the body remain in protest. Let the body
not fall, not yet, not to the ground, to prone
and all its animation taken away by wind
that stirs, that stirs, and won't stir up. Let
not that. Let the jussive command and agree.
Let the mood change and let the square be
as public tonight as are the constellations
of any and all of the gathered.

To be human
is to hold
in one's chest
someone else's
words then say
them again.

To say aloud
an experience
that hasn't
been lived
but now lives
in its saying.

What must be
said can be said
with the body
even in the event
the body has
stilled & cooled.

The human is
the signal within
the noise. Is
touching a receiver.
Wirelessly remote
yet right, right here.

O after, what

                                                       has this changed in you?

            the square is not lyric
            does not operate
            under the conditions
                                         of address, of
                                            the second person.

O, the square is not an apostrophe.
When the words from the square are

                                         you are coming to save us,
                                              aren't you

                                       who are you, there
                                       in the square
                                       out here in a book
                                       some where in the airwaves

        the square is the law   crossing the square diagonally
        is as invisible and
        forgettable as the law   on the way to passing time
        is until the moment
        the citizen is subject   at work, purchasing a coffee.

The square contains itself   and everything inside it
and a poem does not.   O, that a page, that syntax, might recall
        someone to themselves.

ACKNOWLEDGMENTS

The poems in this chapbook were supported by a Project Space residency at the Visual Studies Workshop, Rochester, NY; by a Foundlings Press Artist Residency, Buffalo, NY; and by a Presidential Summer Faculty Fellowship from SUNY Geneseo/The Research Foundation. My lasting gratitude to these organizations for time and space to research, listen, read, write, and share.

Page 1 repurposes and adapts the text of interim Egyptian president Adly Mansour's Law 107, issued November 24, 2013.

Page 12 is a cento using language from *Voices from Tiananmen Square: Beijing Spring and the Democracy Movement*, Ed. Mok Chiu Yu and J. Fran Harrison (Black Rose Books, 1990).

Page 16 takes its words from the index and linked entries for "after" in *Why Occupy a Square: People, Protests and Movements in the Egyptian Revolution* by Jeroen Gunning and Ilan Zvi Baron (Oxford University Press, 2014).

I owe a debt to the found language from a number of sources that enters this chapbook, such as the phrase "who can say who are citizens" (page 3), from Charles Olson's epic poem *Maximus*, and the phrase "you are coming to save us, aren't you" (page 39), overheard on a BBC World Service report from Tahrir Square in 2011. "A world service for men & women so cut off by snow, by desert, by sea, that only voices out of the air could reach them" is how King George V described and imagined the World Service in his first Christmas Message, 19 December 1932.

I am deeply grateful to New Michigan Press for believing in this chapbook and helping the experiences it hopes to document resonate on. This chapbook would also not exist without the words, ideas, and inspiration of so many friends, colleagues, students, writers and fellow travelers—that you are more numerous than there are pages here makes my heart swell. Thank you. Thank you especially to Jess, June, and Rosie: may we always return to each other in words and stories.

Above all, this is for and because of the protestors and refugees, who, among so many other things, gather and travel by and with poems and words. I offer my hands as a cupped bowl for those words.

LYTTON SMITH is the author of the poetry collections *The All-Purpose Magical Tent* and *While You Were Approaching the Spectacle But Before You Were Transformed by It*, both from Nightboat Books, and the chapbooks *Monster Theory* (Poetry Society of America) and *Your Radar Data Knows Its Thing* (Foundlings Press). He is a 2019 NEA Literature Translation Fellowship recipient and the translator of over a dozen novels from the Icelandic; his translations of *Tómas Jónsson, Bestseller* by Guðbergur Bergsson (Open Letter) and *Öræfi* by Ófeigur Sigurðsson (Deep Vellum) were finalists for the Best Translated Book Award in 2018 and 2019 respectively. He is part of the Hostile Environments: Policies, Stories, Responses research group. He lives in western upstate New York where he teaches creative writing, Black Studies, and literature at SUNY Geneseo and serves as the Director of the Center for Integrative Learning.

❂

COLOPHON

Text is set in a digital version of Jenson, designed by Robert Slimbach in 1996, and based on the work of punchcutter, printer, and publisher Nicolas Jenson. The titles here are in Futura.

❊

NEW MICHIGAN PRESS, based in Tucson, Arizona, prints poetry and prose chapbooks, especially work that transcends traditional genre. Together with DIAGRAM, NMP sponsors a yearly chapbook competition.

DIAGRAM, a journal of text, art, and schematic, is published bimonthly at THEDIAGRAM.COM. Periodic print anthologies are available from the New Michigan Press at NEWMICHIGANPRESS.COM.

www.ingramcontent.com/pod-product-compliance
Lightning Source LLC
Chambersburg PA
CBHW080943040426
42444CB00015B/3423